From my family to yours:

This charming tradition began for our family when my children were very small. Like most children through the ages, they wanted to know how Santa really knew who was naughty and who was nice. This answer, as in my own childhood, came in the form of a small Scout Elf.

The first time the Scout Elf arrived at our home, we officially adopted him by giving him a name. In the following years, "Fisbee" would appear around the holidays, usually in late November or early December.

His sole responsibility was to watch over our family daily and report to Santa each night. Upon his return from the North Pole, Fisbee would find a new observation point somewhere in the house. What fun it was to watch the children race each other out of bed every morning to be the first to find him!

In order to preserve the Scout Elf's Christmas magic, our children were not allowed to touch him, but talking to him was definitely encouraged. I can only imagine how many childhood hopes and dreams were shared with Fisbee through the years.

Of course, at that time we didn't know that Fisbee was part of a much bigger story—an enchanted universe dedicated to keeping the spirit of Christmas alive. Just as Santa Claus carries out his mission to share peace and goodwill to all each Christmas Eve, Scout Elves work with him to ensure Christmas cheer stays strong in the hearts of families around the world.

The Santaverse™ world is full of magic and mystery, with stories and characters that reveal how your family and your Scout Elf pal are part of this epic adventure, not only during the holiday season but all year long through the joy and cheer you share with one another.

I never dreamed this simple tradition would lead to so many treasured Christmas memories for our entire family. It is my earnest desire that The Elf on the Shelf® tradition will bring joy to your family, as well.

Enjoy this tradition and make it your own!

With my best wishes for you and those you love,

Carol

Visit elfontheshelf.com/registry to access your Scout Elf's official adoption certificate and a special message from Santa!

The ELF on the SHELF MD/®

A Christmas Tradition

by Carol V. Aebersold and Chanda A. Bell
illustrated by Coë Steinwart

The LumiStella MD® Company

www.lumistella.com

Have you ever wondered how Santa could know
if you're naughty or nice each year as you grow?
For hundreds of years it's been a big secret.
It now can be shared if you promise to keep it.

At holiday time Santa sends me to you.
I watch and report on all that you do.

My job's an assignment from Santa himself.
I am his helper, a friendly Scout Elf.

The first time I come to the place you call home
you quickly must give me a name of my own.

♡Pixie♡

Once you are finished my mission can start.
What will you call me—Sparkle or Heart?
Will it be Foddle, Criddle, or Clyde?
Fisbee's cute, too, but you must decide.

Dec 1ˢᵗ 2024

Fred Markle

zart Fisbee

criddle Ooddle Foddle

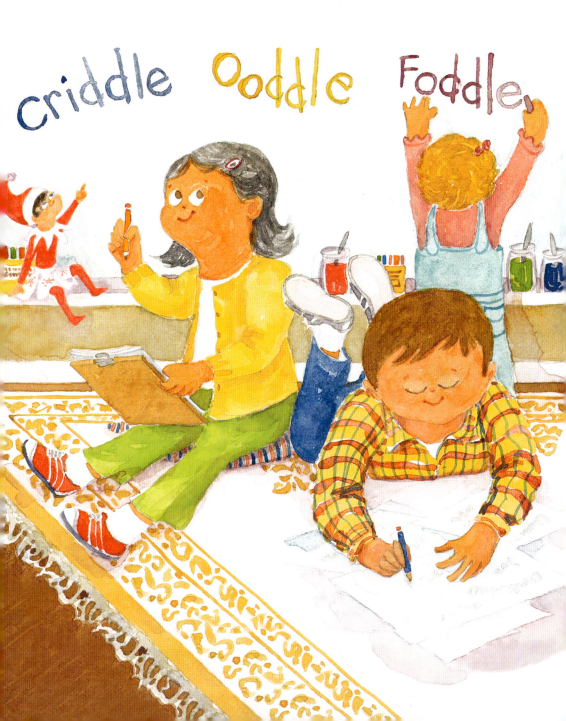

Each night while you're sleeping to Santa I'll fly
to the North Pole right through the dark sky.

Of course Christmas magic helps me to be quick.
I laugh with my friends and report to Saint Nick.

I tell him if you have been good or been bad.
The news of the day makes him happy or sad.
A push or a shove I'll report to "the Boss,"
but small acts of kindness will not be a loss.

In the car, at the park,
or even at school
the word will get out
if you broke a rule.

I'll be back at your home before you awake,
and then you must find the new spot I will take.

You'll jump out of bed and come running to see:
who'll be the first to spy little old me?

Maybe the kitchen, the bathroom, or den
is where you will find me, your special elf friend.
I can hide on a plant, a shelf, or a frame.
Where will I be? Let's make it a game.

There's only one rule that you have to follow
so I will come back and be here tomorrow:

Please do not touch me. My magic might go,
and Santa won't hear all I've seen or I know.

I won't get to tell him that you've said your prayers,
or helped to bake cookies,
or cleaned off the stairs.
How will he know how good you have been?
He might start to think you forgot about him.

I can't speak to you, so says Santa Claus.
All of us elves have to follow his laws.

I'll listen to you. Tell me your wishes.
Would you like a game or some tiny toy dishes?
The gleam in my eye and my bright little smile
shows you I'm listening and noting your file.

The final decision with Santa now rests.
What do you think?
Will you get your request?

The night before Christmas my job's at an end.
The rest of the year with Santa I'll spend.

So blow me a kiss and bid me farewell.
I'll fly away when I hear Santa's bell.
Of course I will miss you,
but wait 'til next year.
When the holidays come I'll again reappear.

Until then I wish every girl and each boy
a Christmas of peace and a year full of joy.

This tradition began for the

_____

family on

_____, 20_____.

We welcomed our Scout Elf
by choosing the name:

_____ .

ISBN: 978-0-9970920-9-7
Printed and bound in China / Imprimé et relié en Chine
9 8 7 6 5 4 3 2 1

www.elfontheshelf.com

THE LUMISTELLA COMPANY
3350 RIVERWOOD PKWY SE, SUITE 300
ATLANTA, GA 30339 USA - É.-U.
+1-877-919-4105 ★ www.lumistella.com